CAVACHON BIBLE AND CAVACHONS

Your Perfect Cavachon Guide

CAVACHONS, CAVACHON DOGS, CAVACHON PUPPIES, CAVACHON TRAINING, CAVACHON NUTRITION, CAVACHON HEALTH, CAVACHON BREEDERS, HISTORY, & MORE!

By Mark Manfield

© DYM Worldwide Publishers, 2019.

I0081190

Published by DYM Worldwide Publishers 2019.

ISBN: 978-1-913154-15-8

Copyright © DYM Worldwide Publishers, 2019
2 Lansdowne Row, Number 240, London W1J 6HL.

Table of Contents

Introduction

Sweet, charming, and family-friendly – these are just a few words to describe the designer breed (or hybrid breed) known as the Cavachon. The Cavachon is the result of breeding the small Cavalier King Charles Spaniel dog with the Bichon Frise. This generally happy pup is reputed to be a great family dog, and although he is descended from hunting dogs (at least partially, anyway), this small designer dog is meant to live indoors with his family. Even so, this little dynamo is full of personality and is happiest when he is given ample opportunities to exercise and socialize. You'll find that the Cavachon loves to be around other people and other dogs, too. The big, adorable eyes of the Cavachon coupled with the soft, wavy fur of the dog's face and ears make the nickname "the teddy bear dog" quite fitting for this designer pooch.

The Cavachon designer dog is a hybrid breed, from a planned breeding of the Cavalier King Charles Spaniel and the Bichon Frise.

You can expect the Cavachon to be a small dog as both parent breeds are small breeds. The Cavachon will have medium-length to long fur, and the ears will be "drop" ears as, once again, both parent breeds share these characteristics. Their hair will typically be wavy, although there are some who have curlier locks. However, the exact look of any Cavachon litter is much like what a breeder expects from a litter of purebred puppies – they generally have their own looks depending upon the exact looks of the pup parents. The Cavalier King Charles Spaniel is known for its gorgeous markings around its ears, eyes, and along its spine and feet. Often, these beautiful markings are present in the Cavachon. The Bichon Frise is often described as white and fluffy. The Cavachon may be one of many colors or color combinations – red, black, sable, blonde and white, tan, or white and a combination of the aforementioned colors.

The Cavachon is typically twenty pounds or less (9.07 kilos or less). Their fur is generally wavy and very soft. In appearance, the Cavachon's fur remains fluffy, giving it the impression of a child's fuzzy teddy bear. Temperament is largely based on the parents of the Cavachon pup, but one can generally expect the Cavachon to desire to spend time with his or her family, enjoy playing with other pups, and overall, being a friendly pup. They are highly social dogs, and they generally make friends with most people and other dogs. In addition, if they are raised around other animals, they tend to accept them into their animal family just as if the animal in question is another Cavachon dog.

Speaking of exercise, the Cavachon does enjoy engaging in fun play, with or without you. The key is making sure that you provide some mentally stimulating toys for times you yourself can't join in playtime. These social dogs can suffer from separation anxiety if they are left alone for long periods of time, so you must consider your personal work schedule as well as other times you tend to be away from home if you are considering bringing a Cavachon home. Cavachons tend to do well with kids and other dogs, in fact, they love the opportunity to play with anyone and everyone! They rarely meet strangers, whether in the animal world or in the human world. They aren't very good at being guard dogs, and, although they will bark, they quickly begin wagging their tails and greeting strangers rather than warning them off.

The Cavachon is noted for its sweet, yet playful nature. This hybrid breed loves people of all ages, but only older children, particularly those who have experience with dogs, should be allowed to play unsupervised with the Cavachon. Younger children may not realize that this small dog can be easily injured by rough play, so until you feel your child is mature enough to play properly with the Cavachon, keep a watchful eye over their play. Don't be fooled – the Cavachon loves boisterous and raucous playtime! However, their small size makes them unsuitable for tight hugs and rowdy behavior that might cause them to be hurt.

The Cavachon will likely have a medium-length, wavy coat of fur. The Cavachon may be the first-generation pup, or it may be an "F2" or second-generation offspring of two Cavachon designer dogs. Either way, your dog may inherit the double coat of the Bichon Frise parent breed. Regardless, the Cavachon will require a moderate amount of grooming in order to prevent developing issues with his skin or coat.

The Cavachon is generally a healthy dog. Both parent breeds are also fairly healthy, and neither parent breed is known for any detrimental health issues. The Bichon Frise may be more prone to issues such as allergies and joint issues, but often, the good health of the Cavalier King Charles Spaniel parent will influence the overall inherited health of the Cavachon. Any pertinent health issues will be discussed in later chapters.

This sweet companion is often touted as being easy to train, particularly where housebreaking is concerned. However, one should remember that the Cavachon might have a bit of an independent streak, and sometimes this requires a little extra patience as the training process takes place. However, if you'll maintain consistency and calm repetition in training, the Cavachon will be trained in no time. The Cavachon is typically extremely bright, so training is fairly easy – provided you insist on consistency and a method of rewarding good behavior. Bringing home a Cavachon is a decision that will be mutually rewarding for both you and your new furry pal.

Ready to embark on your Cavachon journey? It's an adventure that you won't regret!

CHAPTER 1

Cavachon History – Where Did They Come From?

The Cavachon is often referred to as a designer dog, or a hybrid of two breeds purposely allowed to breed in order to create a new "designer" dog. The Cavachon is from a planned breeding of a Cavalier King Charles Spaniel and a Bichon Frise. Because the Cavachon is a mixed breed dog, it is difficult to know exactly what a puppy from this breeding will look like.

The darling Cavachon pup is a mixture of the Cavalier King Charles Spaniel breed and the Bichon Frise breed.

What Is a Cavachon Dog?

We know that the Cavachon is a designer dog or a hybrid breed. Often, with designer dogs, little is known of the origin of the hybrid breed, and enthusiasts must look to the history of the parent breeds to better understand the resulting mix. The designer dog movement can be traced to the early 1990s; with some breeds, the interest in purposely creating a new breed based on crossing two established breeds goes even further back to the 1970s. Overall, we can say that hybrid dogs are definitely twentieth-century creations. With the Cavachon, however, a specific breeder claims that he created the designer breed in 1996. This breeder owns the Gleneden Cavachon breeding facility in

Virginia, and he still raises Cavachons today. However, it is still beneficial to study the history of the two-parent breeds in order to fully understand the origins of the Cavachon.

The Cavalier King Charles Spaniel finds its origins in the United Kingdom. The First Duke of Marlborough, John Churchill, fancied the King Charles Spaniel hunting dog. This dog was a favorite of many royals of the UK, especially King Charles II. In fact, this is the dog's namesake. At one time, particularly around World War II, the dogs faced extinction. It was at this time that a toy spaniel dog was introduced to the breeding line in an effort to recreate the King Charles Spaniel of John Churchill's day. American Roswell Eldridge began this initial effort of attempting to recreate the original King Charles Spaniel. However, Eldridge's attempts to bring back the exact dog that was the companion of the First Duke of Marlborough was never successful. In 1928, the Cavalier King Charles Spaniel breed club was established. It is uncertain how the Cavalier King Charles Spaniel made its way to American shores. Later, the American Kennel Club would accept the breed and create a standard.

Who could resist the sweet face of the Cavachon?

The Bichon Frise' parent breed of the Cavachon designer dog can trace its origins back to France and the Barbet water dog. Bichon Frise' literally means "small, long-haired dog." One of the original Bichon Frise' was a cross between a Poodle and a Maltese. However, many other variations were mixed with the Bichon dog – the Bichon Havanese, Bichon Bolognaise, and the Bichon Tenerife. The Bichon Tenerife is thought to have been so well-liked that this variation is the one that sailors took to various parts of the trading world. The classic book *The Adventures of Tintin* depict a white dog with fluffy hair; the Bichon or a Bichon variation is thought to be the inspiration for this tome. The Bichon Frise' was brought to America in the 1950s – or sometime around then. We do know that the first litter of Bichon Frise' pups in the United States was born in 1956. In 1973, the Bichon Frise' was recognized by the American Kennel Club.

What are Some Cavachon Dog Facts and Cavachon Breed Information?

The Cavachon dog is reputed to be friendly, easy-going, and virtually trouble-free. They don't require a great deal of exercise, nor do they demand a lot of attention. However, the Cavachon is known for following one of his human family members from room to room, eager to be a part of any activity. Some experts recommend purchasing a Cavachon pair, particularly if you work away from home or are otherwise away for several hours each day. The presence of a second pup often soothes any separation anxiety that a solitary Cavachon might experience.

Though the Cavachon does not require a great deal of activity, they DO have a fun energy that makes his family want to engage him in play. Cavachons like to play most any interactive game possible – fetch, chase, or tug of war with a sturdy toy. Although most wouldn't consider the Cavachon a dog that is perfect for hiking or rigorous activities, the Cavachon is good for company while at the beach or walking in the park. Speaking of parks, they do enjoy a visit to the dog park, especially if there are other pups with which to play. The dog park often has a walking track that both you and your Cavachon can utilize, but, there is much more to do there as well! Many dog parks have obstacle courses, which the Cavachon will enjoy traversing with your encouragement. Pet-friendly beaches also provide you and your Cavachon a fun place to play. You might throw a doggy disc to Fido, and a game of fetch on the beach is safe for your Cavachon's joints. As you can see, the Cavachon is a fun-loving dog. If you're active yourself, the Cavachon is a perfect fit to match your energy level. At the same time, the Cavachon also enjoys being a "lap dog," and simply sitting on the couch alongside you. The key to keeping the Cavachon happy and healthy is to ensure that he has at least thirty minutes of daily walk time and plenty of fun toys which he can play with   on his own.

CHAPTER 2

What Do You Need to Know About the Cavachon?

Before bringing home your new Cavachon, there are some factors you should take into consideration. As stated previously, the Cavachon is a joyful dog that will add to any home, but, there may be some situations in which the Cavachon might not be the right fit for your family. Let's discuss important factors about this one-of-a-kind pooch.

The Cavachon is always happy to please its people!

Is the Cavachon Dog Right for my Family?

In the introduction of the book, we discussed the parentage of the Cavachon. Both the Bichon Frise' and the Cavalier King Charles Spaniel are sweet, companionable dogs. This means that chances are the Cavachon offspring will inherit the friendly nature of his or her parents. A good idea, though, is always to visit the breeder's facility and meet the parents of your potential pup. This is the best way to determine if your future pup will have the happy disposition reputed of Cavachons.

The Cavachon is a small dog. He will not be as small and fragile as a Yorkshire Terrier or a Miniature Pinscher, but, still, this is dog will be small. This is important if your family has young children who are not experienced with small dogs. Although most young children mean well, there are reports of dogs becoming injured during rough play with younger, unsupervised children. Therefore, the decision to bring a puppy into a household with small children is yours. If your children will generally be supervised with a small puppy, or if they are obedient when you tell them not to play too rough with a small dog, then the Cavachon should be happy in your home. However, if you do not believe your children are ready for a Cavachon, then wait a few years until they understand that their new pal can be hurt with rough play.

Another consideration involves bringing a new Cavachon pup into a home with other pets. Again, this is often a judgment call on your part. What kind of dogs do you already own? Or do you own cats? How many other animals do you already own? Generally, the Cavachon is happy-go-lucky and gets along with other dogs and cats too! However, you might want to think about the animals you already own. Do they tend to accept other animals? Are they friendly? Do your current animals demand a good bit of your attention? Now, it must be stated that Cavachons do enjoy the company of other dogs, especially if you are away from home due to work or school for several hours each day. If you believe your older dogs will accept the new puppy and enjoy a friendship with the Cavachon, then, by all means, the Cavachon will likely fit into your home dynamic very well. If you have cats, they may be a little wary of your new fuzzy pal. The best way to gauge this is to have a friend bring over a similar dog and expose your cat to the dog. Watch your feline's reaction. If he or she seems unaffected, likely your kitty won't be too bothered by the presence of a new pup. If your cat (or cats) have grown up around dogs, then they probably won't notice a new addition. Remember that Cavachons have a tendency to enjoy the company of other animals, and, if they are raised with other dogs and cats (or birds, or virtually any other animal), they will adapt and be happy pups.

Some potential owners are unsure of whether they should choose a male or female Cavachon. This is chiefly a personal preference. Intact males of all dog breeds have a tendency to mount or mark their territory. (Intact means that the dog is not neutered and still able to mate with a female.) Neutering a puppy as soon as the vet says it's safe can prevent this behavior. Females that are not intended for breeding should be spayed as soon as the vet gives the go-ahead also as they can experience phantom pregnancies, plus, when she does experience going into heat for the first time, she may become a little aggressive. In addition, you'll have to separate her from any intact males, and you'll have to clean up any discharge that is a part of the heat cycle. (Note: There are products available that can help you prevent discharge from getting on furniture or other surfaces. Much like a child's diaper, these specially-made pants for females in heat can be purchased at a pet store for a nominal price.) Again, spaying the female as soon as the vet says it's safe to do so will keep you from experiencing this on a regular basis. Therefore, the gender you choose is completely up to you.

Although we will discuss the overall costs associated with the Cavachon later, you do need to consider the initial cost of a Cavachon and the regular costs associated with owning this hybrid breed. You'll need to consider not only the purchase price of your new pup but also any costs associated with purchasing the accessories your Cavachon will need to come home with you. You'll also need to consider veterinarian costs, the cost of food, and the possible microchipping of your pup. Don't forget grooming costs – the Cavachon will need some grooming, even if you purchase the brushes and clippers to groom your pup yourself. As dogs go, the Cavachon is not an overly expensive dog to own. However, it is best to be informed about the possible costs going into the decision.

Finally, the Cavachon is a friendly dog that enjoys spending time with you and your family. With proper supervision, the Cavachon does well with children of all ages. This pooch does not require a lot of exercise, but they do enjoy attention from their family members. Therefore, they may experience separation anxiety if you tend to be away from home for hours at a time most every day. You may consider purchasing two Cavachon if this might be an issue. Cavachon dogs tend to get along with other dog breeds, and they also get along with cats and other animals. Although there are some costs associated with owning a Cavachon, these are not outrageous. All in all, these are important factors to consider when thinking about purchasing a Cavachon.

What is the Average Life Expectancy of the Cavachon?

The Cavachon has an average life expectancy of twelve years. They can live anywhere from ten years to fifteen years, however. This will depend on the health of the individual dog. Furthermore, many Cavachons live a certain number of years based on the genetics of the parent dogs. Your breeder may have some information about the immediate relatives of the puppy you are considering, particularly if they have raised the parents of the litter and those pup parents before that.

It should be stated that if you keep the Cavachon healthy by getting all vaccinations, keeping regular check-up appointments at the vet, and by providing a healthy diet throughout the years, the Cavachon may live longer than the average life span. In chapter 12, we will discuss the "golden years" of your Cavachon's life and the health issues that might be present at that time as well as the care you should provide a senior Cavachon dog.

Can You Describe the Typical Behavior of a Cavachon dog? Do They Get Along with Cats?

The Cavachon is a laid-back dog with a people-pleasing attitude. Provided you give the Cavachon proper socialization, the Cavachon will get along with all types of animals and people of all ages. They do like to interact with their humans, though, so remember that regular activity each day, even for only thirty minutes to an hour, will go far in making sure Fido works out any nervous energy. For those who are away or may not be able to take the dog for long walks each day, providing the Cavachon with toys that stimulate them mentally – food puzzle toys, for instance – will keep them occupied and will keep them from becoming bored. Just as it holds with other dog breeds, the Cavachon will chew or otherwise misbehave if he is left for long periods alone and without the company of another pup or human family member.

As previously stated, the Cavachon will get along with cats as long as he is socialized from a young age. Socialization is a natural part of training your Cavachon, which will be discussed later in the book. Socializing a Cavachon to a cat can take place in a few different ways. In the best-case scenario, you could raise a Cavachon and a kitten together. In this case, the pooch and the cat wouldn't even realize that they're different species. However, you may find yourself wishing to bring a kitten home after you've had a Cavachon for a few years. To gauge how well your Cavachon will get along with a cat, enlist the help of a friend who has a friendly feline. Take your Cavachon over a few times a week and allow the two to play together. Once you have determined that your pup will tolerate cats, find a friend who has a kitten and allow the two to hang out. This will give the Cavachon ample opportunities to get socialized to cats.

Remember, puppies are the most adaptable. So, you shouldn't worry too much about placing a puppy and an adult cat together. Definitely supervise them for the first few days, as your cat may hiss or swat at the new puppy. Over time, however, most cats will adapt to a new puppy, especially if they are younger adult cats.

This Cavachon has a fairly short haircut.

CHAPTER 3

Cavachon Breeders – What Are The Things You Need to Keep in Mind?

The first step in bringing home a happy, healthy Cavachon pup is researching potential breeders from which to purchase your new dog. Yes, researching! Coupled with visiting potential breeders, researching the breeders near you is the most important step in finding a healthy Cavachon pup to add to your family. It is common knowledge that there are unscrupulous backyard breeders who exploit the dogs under their care for profit. There are also those who would scam innocent people out of their money in the form of deposits. In this chapter, we will discuss the signs of a disreputable breeder just as we will point out the marks of a breeder who loves the breed and treats their breeding stock as a part of the family, the way a pet parent should. Follow us as we look at finding a reputable Cavachon breeder.

The Cavachon often acts as a model puppy in photography.

Cavachon Breeders Near Me – What are the Signs of a Good Breeder?

Likely you've seen commercials for animal rescue organizations in which mistreated dogs are housed in makeshift dog houses, some chained to the structure, without water or proper bedding. Some are starving; they may have matted fur, and they may suffer from a wide range of health ailments. This is the stereotypical image of the breeder for profit. However, not all breeding mills are this obvious. This is why you'll need to arm yourself with certain knowledge that will allow you to discern between good breeders and those who have no real concern other than making money.

Let me first say that at the end of this book, located in a bonus chapter, there will be a list of breeders across the United States and the United Kingdom as well as Canada. So, you won't have to start from scratch on finding breeders. However, it is up to you to make contact with the breeders and start a conversation regarding their pups, prices, and a little more in-depth information regarding their breeding facilities.

You'll want to take time to talk with the breeder in order to get an idea of their beliefs regarding breeding. There are those breeders who only allow their breeding stock to have one or two litters per year. This is so they can protect the health of the mother. Pregnancy depletes her body of many vitamins and minerals, and failure to allow her to replenish those vital nutrients compromises not only her health but the health of future pups as well. Those breeders who have multiple litters per year aren't necessarily breeding mills, either. There are those breeders who have several mother dogs, and they plan for the litters each year based upon the estrus cycle of each mother as well as their ability to tend to each litter as it is born and raised to the point that the pups are adoptable. However, there are breeders who have multiple litters per year without any regard for the health of the mothers or the pups. The best way to gauge this is to ask questions about breeding policy and how many times a year a mother dog is allowed to have pups.

An ethical breeder will be proactive in asking you questions too! This is because they are not as concerned about profit as they are making sure the puppies raised in their care find loving homes. You may find that the breeder asks that you wait until the puppy is between eight to ten weeks of age before you pick the puppy up. The breeder will also ask general questions about you, your family, and your experience with dogs. If you have children, the breeder may ask about their experience with dogs, especially small dogs. Don't be surprised if you are asked about your children's experience with small dogs. An ethical breeder is intent on protecting the breed, and he or she wants to ensure that the puppies sold go to good homes. Don't be surprised if a breeder tells you that he or she won't sell to anyone with children under a certain age. Again, this is protection for the pups and a sign that the breeder does everything possible to ensure their pups go to good homes.

An ethical breeder may ask you about your home, your work, and your daily routine. He or she may ask about other pets in the home. Again, this is proof that the breeder has the best interest of the puppies at heart.

Ethical breeders may have invested in genetic testing of their breeding stock, and they will be able to provide proof of said testing to you. They are also likely to have records of the parent dogs' veterinarian visits, including shot records, proof of worming, and other routine care procedures typical of breeding stock. A reputable breeder will not allow a dog that has tested positive for genetic problems to be used for breeding. Don't be shy about asking for this proof. Many small dogs have genetic issues such as hip dysplasia or eye conditions. Ask the breeder specifically if the parents have undergone genetic testing for these issues, and ask if you'll be provided proof of that when you pick up the puppy. Should the breeder shy away from this even after stating that the parents have undergone genetic testing, then it is likely the breeder isn't being quite truthful.

One expert says that you might feel as if you are the one being interviewed when you speak with a potential breeder. This is also a sign of a good breeder who has only the health of the dogs in mind. In addition to questions about your family and your home, the ethical breeder might ask about your own experience with dogs. Don't be upset if you're a first-time pet parent; this won't disqualify you from being sold a puppy. The Cavachon is a great breed for novice dog owners, and the breeder knows this. An experienced breeder will know that you have the best interest of the Cavachon at heart, and he or she will take this into consideration. The breeder may speak with you about your routine, and he or she may caution you about leaving the Cavachon at home for long periods of time. Remember the Cavachon may suffer from separation anxiety if he is left alone for long periods of time without much human interaction. The breeder knows this and will inquire as to how you intend to prevent this issue.

Although you are right to be wary of a breeder you've only spoken with over the phone, the fact that there ARE puppy mills out there that will exploit a dog give you plenty of reason to be skeptical. Some puppy mill owners can pass the over-the-phone interview, but they'll throw some red flags when you ask to come to visit their facilities.

That's right – one of the best things you can do is take time to visit the breeding facilities. Now, don't assume that you should expect to see a fancy facility. Some hobbyist breeders have a space in the home for the one of two litters they might raise each year. As long as the space is clean, this is perfectly acceptable. Speaking of cleanliness, this is the first sign you might be dealing with a disreputable breeder. Not only should the space in which the puppies are occupying be clean, but the puppies and their parents should also be. With the Cavachon, grooming might not be recently completed, but their fur should be free of matting. They should be curious about you, the visitor. Barking is normal, of course, but the Cavachon never meets a stranger, so he should approach you for a little attention. Even if the dogs seem a little shy, they should not appear skittish. Unwillingness to interact with humans might be a sign that the dogs don't live in a positive environment.

NOTE: Some mother dogs are a little less friendly when they have a litter of puppies to care for. They are like all animal mothers – they protect their young first and foremost. If the mom doesn't try to interact much, but other dogs on the premises are friendly, then you can reasonably deduce that Mama Cavachon is just protecting her babies, a very natural reaction to strangers. Older puppies, however, that are walking around and becoming more independent from their moms, will likely come to you as they are already getting lots of attention from the breeder's family and the breeder.

Another tale-tell sign that you might be encountering an unethical breeder is, upon visiting the facility, finding several different breeds of dog on the premises (all available for sale, of course). It's not uncommon for a reputable breeder to have two litters whelp at the same time, but most breeders know that their mother dogs must have special attention during pregnancy and whelping, in addition to afterward when they are caring for a litter. Plus, many reputable breeders will sit up with the mother when she is whelping, and they also know that, if something happens, they will have to bottle feed the puppies. In other words, a reputable breeder generally plans the litters based upon the time their females go into season, and they do everything possible to make sure that if there are multiple breeding females, they do not all have litters within the same time period. They know they may need to provide specialized care, and so, they plan the litters as carefully as possible.

Do not be drawn in by a cheap price. A reputable breeder will set a price based on veterinary care, quality of food provided, and the cost of any genetic testing they might have had to carry out in order to determine if a dog is healthy enough for breeding stock. Take the English or French Bulldog, for example. The breeder knows that the veterinarian will need to provide a great deal of care for the mother both prior to and during the birth of the puppies. A good breeder will gladly provide this care, but the cost is usually passed on to the consumer. While the Cavachon mother might not need the assistance of the vet during the whelping process, a good breeder will still make sure the mother visits the vet as needed during her pregnancy. The reputable breeder will take the puppies at two weeks and at four weeks for vet visits, and the reputable breeder will provide the buyer evidence of vaccinations, worming, and other well-care documentation upon request. Conversely, an astronomical price for a Cavachon pup isn't necessary, either. The average price of a Cavachon based upon research is roughly $800, but prices may range from half that price to upwards of $6,000.

Cheap prices don' t always mean you aren't getting a quality dog (a hobbyist may not charge a large price for a Cavachon, but they still provide great care and plenty of veterinarian care as well). However, buying the most expensive pup doesn't mean that you are getting a healthy pup either. Use a combination of interviewing and talking with the breeder as well as a visit to the facility to determine if the breeders you are considering are truly ethical and reputable. You will know most of the time if the breeder has the best interest of the pups at heart.

A word about deposits – I personally have read many horror stories of people speaking with a breeder over the phone, then sending a deposit via an online payment service. Be careful of this practice. Many services will not refund your money if it is discovered that the money you sent to a breeder was for a deposit on a pet. Furthermore, there are those inscrutable people who would ask you to send the money and to describe the transaction as if you are sending the money "to a friend" so that you will not be charged fees. Again, most services' policies will not refund your money if you follow these directives from the breeder.

With deposits, it really is best to be sure that the puppies have already been born, and that there is a contract between you and the breeder. The breeder has the right to state "no refunds" as far as the deposit goes. However, you are under no obligation to sign this contract. You can ask to have in the contract that if the breeder does not produce a puppy for you, what recourse you'll have. The contract can state that in the event the puppy promised to you dies or otherwise becomes unavailable, you are entitled to a refund or a puppy from a later litter. It is difficult to determine if a breeder is reputable when so many transactions take place online, and you may not always live near the breeder so that you can actually visit the facility and hand the breeder a deposit in the form of a check or money order. However, you can still send a money order or a cashier's check, which you will have some ability to recoup if the breeder does not provide you with a pup. Be aware that you might have to take the breeder to small claims court to do so, but, at least you will have some way to get a refund. Remember, most services will NOT cover refunding a deposit on a live animal, so do not allow yourself to be bullied into sending a deposit electronically. Finally, keep the contract handy. In the highly unlikely situation that the agreement between you and the breeder falls through, you want to have proof of your claim to a puppy and the deposit you paid.

If you'll notice, the advice to visit the breeder is repeated throughout the previous chapters. There is a reason for this. It is very important, especially if the breeder is located within traveling distance, for you to visit the breeding facilities. The breeder should have no problem introducing you to the mother dog, and you should be able to view where the puppies are kept. A definite red flag should be the breeder offering only to meet you somewhere with the puppies. A stressed-out mom – and stress can be caused by poor diet as well as cramped and dirty living conditions – will give birth to stressed out pups. Unfortunately, the negative behavior that often results from these detrimental early beginnings does not show itself until the puppy has gotten into the "adolescent" stage or perhaps even when it is older (during adulthood). Again, a reputable breeder will want to do everything possible to secure the best future for any pups they raise. A breeder who is interested only for profit will not care about the pups' living situation or what their future health will be like. They are simply interested in making money.

Another warning sign you should note is a breeder who is willing to let a puppy go before the youngster is eight to ten weeks old. Puppies at one time were allowed to be separated from their mothers at six weeks of age. We know today that it is best for the puppy to stay with its mother until he or she is at least eight weeks old. The puppy will have a better start in life if allowed to do so, and he or she will also have the opportunity to be completely weaned and accustomed to eating solid food.

Previously, we discussed the idea that the breeder should interview you much the same way that you interview him or her. They should ask questions about children in the home, whether you have any experience as a pet parent, and about your typical daily schedule. You may even be asked to present a veterinarian reference. Any and all of these questions you should welcome as this means the breeder is concerned about the welfare of the pups not only while they are under his or her care, but also as they grow into adults in their forever homes.

What are the average prices of a Cavachon dog?

Depending upon where you are located, a Cavachon dog can possess an initial cost ranging from $765 to $2000 (1,530 to 4,000 euro). Again, this is only the initial cost to purchase the pup. Some experts suggest that you budget for *bringing the Cavachon pup home* at a cost of $700 - $6300 (623.67 euro to 5613.15 euro). This includes the cost of the pup plus the initial acquisition of toys, food, bedding, a kennel, and other necessities that your new Cavachon pup will need.

Should I Buy a Cavachon Puppy or an Adult Cavachon Dog?

First, let me begin by saying that this is a very personal choice. Let's take a look at your lifestyle.

Are you away from home a good bit? Do you lead an active lifestyle? Are you willing to take the time to housebreak a puppy properly? Will you take the time to puppy-proof your home so that he or she does not get into mischief that can cause harm? Do you really have the patience to deal with a young puppy? This may seem harsh, but answering these questions honestly will help you to make the right decision about the dog you intend to bring home.

Let's talk about bringing an adult Cavachon into your home. You'll need to make sure that you keep things quiet, and introduce the dog to your routine slowly. With adult dogs, you may have issues getting them to trust you. They may have undesirable habits which you will need to help them break and adopt more acceptable behavior. Now, not all adult dogs have "something wrong" with them in order to be sold by the original owner. However, always approach a dog you do not know with the idea that you need to take things slowly when introducing the adult Cavachon into your home.

At the same time, there are plenty of adult Cavachons that have been rehomed because the original owner might be moving to a place where pets are not allowed or for some other unpreventable reason. The Cavachon may have been very loved prior to being rehomed. In this case, the adult Cavachon you bring home may be rather happy-go-lucky. However, even the happiest dogs may experience separation anxiety when being rehomed. They may bark at night, and don't be surprised if the adult appears to bare her teeth at you for a few days. In this case, give the dog a few days to become accustomed to you and your family. One expert states that she goes on about her routine and often acts as if there is no new dog in her home when bringing in a foster or rescue. After a day or two, the foster accepts that this is a safe place, and they drop a lot of the anxiety that they may have when first trying to acclimate to a new home.

Remember, either of these choices will require you to really think about what changes you are willing to make to your lifestyle in order to properly incorporate a dog. Consider what you are willing to change to accommodate a dog, and then you'll make the right decision regarding what age pup you will be bringing home.

Should I Foster a Cavachon?

If you have experience with dogs, and you think this might help in your decision to purchase an adult Cavachon or a puppy, then, by all means, definitely consider fostering! Fostering a dog is a lot like bringing home an adult dog permanently. You will need to remember that the dog may have been in a not-so-desirable living situation. You may find that the foster dog is overwhelmed by consistent attention and affection. For this reason, you might need to, in a way, "ignore" the dog. Bring the foster dog home, allow him or her to explore and make adjustments on his or her own time. In time, the foster will learn that he or she can trust you, and you can be more affectionate with the dog.

You should ask the rescue or animal shelter with whom you partner to foster dogs a few questions. First, you need to know how long you'll be expected to foster the dog, who is responsible for any expenses related to the care of the dog, procedures for handling a veterinary emergency, what to do if the Cavachon you're fostering is adopted, and whether or not you will be able to adopt the fostered Cavachon if no one else chooses to adopt the dog.

Again, you must answer some tough questions about yourself. If you are likely to get attached to the dog, and the foster Cavachon is adopted, will you be able to deal with giving the dog up? If you feel that you might become too attached to the foster, then you can always volunteer to keep dogs for a short period of time. Fosters are always needed in situations where the pet foster parent keeps a dog for a weekend or just a few days before a dog can be picked up or delivered to its forever home. This will provide you with the experience of interacting with an older Cavachon without the possibility of your bonding closely with the foster. Another possibility regarding rescue and fostering has to do with helping to transport rescue dogs from the rescue to adoptive families. For instance, if a rescue dog is located in Florida, but the family approved to adopt him is located in Texas, a volunteer might be asked to help with transporting the dog. Others are asked to accept the "foster" for a few nights during the transport until another runner can pick the dog up and finish the process of transporting him. These are great ways to ease yourself into the possibility of fostering or owning an adult dog rather than starting with a puppy.

Next, if you aren't very experienced with dogs, fostering – especially if the dog has behavioral problems – might not be a good decision. The majority of Cavachons are sweet, happy pups, but a dog that has been through a lot of trauma and stress may not have the common disposition of a Cavachon. You certainly don't want to form an opinion regarding this wonderful breed based on a dog who has had a hard life and might not know how to accept affection from a loving family. If you do decide to foster a Cavachon, then remember he or she may need a little time to adjust, and slowly, but surely, the foster will begin to respond to your love and care.

CHAPTER 4

Cavachon Adoption – What are Crucial Things to Consider?

We have discussed whether you should choose a Cavachon puppy or an adult dog when buying a Cavachon. We've even broached the idea of fostering a Cavachon that is looking for its forever home. However, if you believe that you might be up to the challenge of bringing an adult Cavachon home, then you should consider adopting a Cavachon.

Keep in mind that there are some Cavachons up for adoption that may not have reached full adulthood. They may be between six and twenty-four months of age. At the same time, dogs up for adoption may be senior adult dogs (ten years plus). They may be owner surrenders (perhaps the owner is an older adult who had to move to a retirement community that does not allow for pets). Not all dogs who are up for adoption have suffered a hardscrabble life. However, you should prepare yourself for any possibility. Older dogs can still be great companions. The younger dogs being placed for adoption may still be highly trainable. There are many advantages to adopting a Cavachon, so let's explore whether this is an option for you.

The Cavachon is an adorable dog that is a great addition to any home.

Cavachon Dog Rescue – Grown Cavachon Adoption

Many individuals are now considering adopting dogs rather than utilizing the puppy mills that so often turn out pups that may end up in a pet store or sold via social media sites. Even so, most people still want a puppy that they have raised and trained to fit their family's lifestyle. Yet, you should consider adopting a dog, even an adult Cavachon, from a rescue or shelter.

Previously, we discussed many of the pitfalls of bringing home an adult dog, particularly one that has not had a good life prior to coming home with you. However, don't let this keep you from considering an adult adoption. There are many, many testimonials across the globe of rescue dogs who have rewarded their forever families many times over just for accepting them into the family. Much of this is due to how you work with an adopted adult in the first days you bring the dog into your home. Remember to give him time to become acclimated to you, your family, and your routine. Dogs who have had a difficult early life often need just a little extra time to trust new owners, but one caveat of choosing a Cavachon adult dog to adopt is the fact that Cavachons naturally love their humans and crave an affectionate relationship with them. So, even if you have to give Fido time to understand that he is in a loving forever home, it will be well worth the time and space necessary to garner his trust.

What are some other advantages to adopting a Cavachon? First, adoption fees are often astronomically lower when compared to the initial purchase price of a Cavachon pup. Depending upon your location, you may pay no more than $200 (130 euro) to adopt a dog. Often, this includes vaccinations, the spaying or neutering of the dog, and other health treatments such as worming the dog. When you compare this to the purchase price of a puppy plus paying individually for the aforementioned services, then you will see that adopting a Cavachon of any age is often much cheaper than purchasing a young puppy.

Next, some adult Cavachons up for adoption are already housebroken. Keep in mind that some adult dogs in a shelter may be owner surrenders, and the owner may have had to surrender the dog for some honorable reasons, such as an older adult who must move into a retirement community or who have experienced health issues that prevent them from properly caring a dog. These dogs are often great adoption candidates. Bonus points if the dog was also trained in obedience by their former owner.

Finally, consider that adopting an adult dog and buying a new puppy are in some ways much the same. Just as you do not know what the temperament of a puppy will be – and remember, you may not know what a puppy's real temperament is until the puppy is a year old or older – you cannot always tell if an adult dog in the shelter possesses a bad personality. Keep in mind that dogs in a shelter are often frightened. They do not know why they have been put into a cage with strange people and strange dogs. This is especially true if a dog has been surrendered to a shelter in the hopes someone will come along and adopt them. However, once again, I point to testimonials of dogs who just seem to communicate to the right person that comes along, "Hey! I'm a happy, loving dog! I want to be a part of your family!" This is what proponents of adoption mean when they say that you can't always tell the future temperament of a puppy, but with an adult dog, what you see is what you get.

NOTE: Some adult dogs that may be adopted are rehomed by their original owners, not sent to a shelter. Perhaps the adult child of an elderly person who knows that Mom or Dad can no longer properly care for a dog is rehoming the pooch. This is a great way to find an adult dog to adopt; they have been cared for and know love. Given time to adjust to a new family, they will make great additions to your home!

How Do I Find Cavachon Dogs for Adoption?

Are you on social media? Many Facebook groups that cater to those who are looking for certain breeds of dogs. Often, these groups are set up for members in a certain locality; if you live in Virginia (the United States), there are groups set up for people who live in or near that state. Become a member of these groups, and often, you'll see listings of dogs whose families may need to rehome them.

Also, there are a number of rescues and adoption centers across the United States. Most of these organizations cater to all types of dogs, but, if you check often, you may find a Cavachon for adoption. You can also establish contact with the people who run the shelters and ask to be put on a waiting list for a Cavachon dog. It's important to reach out and make contacts so that you can find the perfect adoption dog for you. Furthermore, a list of these types of facilities can be found in the bonus chapter of this book.

For those in Canada or the United Kingdom, a list of rescues and adoption centers will also be included in the bonus chapter.

You can also post a notice at your veterinarian's office. Some vets have a bulletin board that features puppies for sale or dogs that need to be rehomed. Every once in a while, you may find a dog that has been surrendered to the veterinarian, so don't hesitate to speak with your veterinarian on helping you keep an eye out for possible adoption opportunities.

Is there a Cavachon Rescue Centre Near Me?

You can always do a simple search to look for Cavachon rescue organizations, no matter where you are located. Keep in mind that you may have to also search for animal rescues that cater to all breeds of dogs as the Cavachon is a designer breed and the demand for a rescue that caters solely to the Cavachon may not be enough to warrant a rescue devoted to the breed. It should be noted that while researching for this book, the writer often found searching for small-breed rescues to be a bonus in finding a Cavachon.

Check the bonus chapter for a list of adoption centers across the United States, Canada, and the United Kingdom.

Other Adoption Considerations

Although this piece of wisdom may seem like a no-brainer, you need to consider your current living conditions and the space you have for a dog. Although the Cavachon is small and generally just as happy in an apartment as he is in a larger home, you should think about a place for the new dog to play. The Cavachon needs exercise, whether you play fetch indoors, or you take a trip to the dog park multiple times each week. The ideal living situation includes a place with a fenced-in yard where you can let the Cavachon get outside and burn off some of that energy. However, if you live in an area where this is not possible, you can provide the Cavachon with toys that encourage mental stimulation. You might even consider mixing in a few toys that allow the Cavachon to chew as needed – this is especially important for younger Cavachons as their teeth come in.

Regardless of your living space, provide the new Cavachon with an area all her own, including her bedding, toys, and anything else she might need to feel secure. The yard is a bonus, but don't let that prevent you from adopting a great dog should you live in an apartment or in an area where you do not have an enclosed play area for your new fur baby.

Next, take a good look at yourself and your family. Although it's been my experience that kids and pets should grow up together, there are many experts who recommend waiting until your child is at least seven years of age. However, young children can be taught to respect a dog and its boundaries; furthermore, a young child who is supervised with a small Cavachon can bond with the dog. Eventually, the child will understand that he or she cannot squeeze the Cavachon too tightly or play too roughly. And, I want to caution you – if your child is not up for the responsibility just yet, you may very well need to wait until the child is mature enough to understand that a dog the size of the Cavachon can be injured if care is not taken.

Then, you'll want to consider your own lifestyle. Do you travel with work? Is your family active? Do you like to take trips often, or at the spur of the moment? Then maybe you should consider whether bringing a Cavachon is right for you. Cavachons can suffer from separation anxiety, so think carefully about whether you are willing to change your lifestyle in order to bring this wonderful dog into your home. One way to combat this is to purchase or adopt two Cavachons at the same time. They will keep one another company while you are away at work.

Cavachon puppies tend to get into mischief when left alone!

If you live an active lifestyle, there's no reason that the Cavachon cannot be a part of that. Many public places are more than willing to allow dogs in with their humans. Did you know that many restaurants are now providing an outdoor dining area so that canines can enjoy a lunch date with their human family? Or that many outdoor markets allow dogs to accompany their owners as they shop? These are just two places that you can take Fido where he was not allowed before! If you enjoy the park, your Cavachon will too! The beach? The Cavachon loves to play fetch on the sand (which provides a great place to run and play without impacting their joints detrimentally). Do you like to travel? Plan ahead, and you can not only make sure Fido has accommodations with you at the hotel, but you can also plan to take him on a variety of activities in your destination city. NOTE: If you are going to a place where taking your dog along is ill-advised, then you should not take Fido on that vacation. Even if you leave him in your hotel room, unsavory individuals can break in and take the dog while you are out with your family. The best advice is to board him with a trusted individual who will provide him with exercise, food, and the feeling of having a home away from home.

Although you might be attracted to adopting a dog because of the lower initial costs, you need to consider other costs associated with bringing your dog home. Toys, travel crates as well as a kennel, regular veterinarian health care, leashes, collars or harnesses, food, and many other accessories that will be necessary to keep your dog happy and healthy can add up over time. Will your budget allow for these items?

Although it might seem that there is much to consider when adopting a Cavachon, the reward you receive from bringing this special designer dog home far outweigh any changes in lifestyle you might need to make. It's important to remember that a dog is a big responsibility, but it is one that gives back to the pet parent exponentially.

CHAPTER 5

Cavachon Supplies – What Do You Need?

S o, you've decided that your life will be better for having a Cavachon in it. Now, it's time to bring Baby home! But, first, what will the new pooch need in order to be happy and feel at home with you?

You will need to purchase a few things to make life for your Cavachon happier and healthier.

Previously, we discussed things such as a crate, kennel, toys, food, and vet care, but we should also consider clothing (yes, some pet parents like to dress the adorable Cavachon for outings), treats, pet health insurance, food and water bowls, a dog bed, and a leash and collar. These are some of the accessories that you may need to purchase for Fido's health and happiness. Let's discuss the items, why you might need them, and the possibility of costs associated with them.

Cavachon Dog Toys

If you are bringing home a dog of any age, you should invest in a few sturdy toys that will provide mental stimulation to the Cavachon. For puppies, chew toys will help to prevent them from destroying shoes, furniture, and more. You can invest in a natural chew toy, such as a cow hoof. These chew toys cost little and last for quite some time. They really help pups to feed their craving for chewing, but they will not damage the pup's teeth. There are also chew toys which are durable and soothing to the tender gums of a teething pup. Some individuals also purchase chew toys that help to clean their dog's teeth. There are some good products on the market, but be sure to read the reviews before purchasing one of these.

One chew toy that you might want to consider should you be away from home a good bit is a food puzzle toy. Food puzzle toys have openings in which you can put small treats or peanut butter inside. Fido must then shake, chew, lick, or even toss the toy in order to get the reward of food. This helps the dog to satisfy those instincts belonging to the dog's ancestors – the ones in which dogs and their wolf ancestors had to work to get food rather than simply walk up to a food bowl. The dog will have to "think" about how to get the food inside the toy, and this gives them the mental stimulation we've discussed previously. Giving the Cavachon something to "do" while you are away prevents the aforementioned separation anxiety and boredom, which can prompt Fido to be disobedient, chew, or otherwise behave negatively.

You will also want a few toys for the Cavachon so that you can play with him. A ball, a Frisbee especially made for dogs (called a doggy disc), and a flirt pole will all allow you to interact with your Cavachon and form that special bond that he so desires. Each of these toys is relatively cheap and can be found in any pet supply store.

Other Cavachon Supplies

When considering your Cavachon's sleeping arrangements, you will need to decide whether your puppy will sleep in a kennel or in a doggy bed. NOTE: Be forewarned – you may need to resign yourself to the idea that the pup may want to sleep on a blanket even if you've purchased the best bed for its sleeping pleasure. However, this is not something that you can predict. It's best to buy a bed that is not very expensive to see if your dog will enjoy the bed. He or she may just want to sleep on a fluffy blanket in his kennel. You can always upgrade to a better bed if you see that your dog likes sleeping in a bed. We'll discuss the best beds later in this chapter.

Consider food and water bowls. You may buy individual bowls, or you may decide to purchase a gravity-fed feeding/watering system. You should also note that there are electronic feeding/

watering systems that can also serve your purposes well. Individuals bowls are good for when you are home a good bit of the time, and you are able to maintain the water and food as needed. Gravity-fed bowls are great for watering your dog, especially if you tend to be away from home during the day. A gravity-fed water bowl will ensure that your dog does not run out while you are working or running errands. Gravity-fed feeding bowls are another issue. These are not necessary, but more of a personal preference. Make sure that you keep the gravity-fed watering and feeding bowls clean and sanitary. Electronic feeding and watering bowls are a great idea if you are away a good bit. However, concerning the watering bowl, you can purchase a gravity-fed water bowl much cheaper than the electronic version, and it works much the same way. The electronic feeding bowl, however, can be a really great asset if you want to ensure that your pup has ample food at certain times during the day. The electronic feeding bowl can be programmed to release a certain amount of food at certain times of the day. If you have a varying work schedule, or you have times when you are away during what would be the feeding time, then investing in the electronic feeding bowl is a great decision. Again, make sure that you clean the bowls regularly so that no bacteria is allowed to grow in the containers.

Next, you'll need to purchase a collar or harness and a leash for your puppy. A puppy needs a small leash, and you'll likely have to get a slightly larger leash in a month or two. In fact, you'll probably need to resign yourself to having to buy several collars before your Cavachon is fully grown. An alternative (but still an item you'll need to replace a few times due to the puppy's growth) is a harness. I prefer a harness to a collar for a number of reasons. First, a collar is cute, but, if your dog is allowed to go into her kennel with the collar on, she can get the collar caught on something and injure herself. (NOTE: You can prevent this by always removing the collar.) Collars may not be as conducive to training your pup as a harness. If your Cavachon tends to pull at the leash, a collar can damage the windpipe of your dog. A harness will leave the neck and windpipe clear. In fact, you can purchase a harness that controls pulling in order to break your pooch from this potentially dangerous habit. Another great perk of using a harness is that you can leave your pup in the harness for hours at a time. (NOTE: It is recommended that you remove the harness a few times a week – perhaps at night – so that the harness does not chafe your pup's front legs. You should also wash it regularly.) When considering leashes, you'll need a short leash for a young dog. Leashes longer than six feet may be utilized after your puppy is trained to walk with you (after the age of two).

The travel crate is an important accessory. You will have opportunities to travel with your Cavachon, and, while it might seem easier just to put your dog in your car, it is safer for you to use a travel crate and secure the crate as you travel. Because the Cavachon is not a large dog even when fully grown, you can buy a smaller crate for your purposes. You also can likely use this same travel kennel as long as it lasts because even a grown Cavachon will fit perfectly in a small travel crate.

This small crate is perfect for traveling with any size Cavachon from a puppy to adulthood.

Another type of crate or kennel that you'll definitely need to purchase is a wire kennel. Now, you CAN get a larger version of the kennel pictured above to keep the puppy in at night or while you're away. However, it's my experience that the wire kennel pictured below is the best choice for a dog living indoors. Let's explore why.

A wire kennel with a removable tray is best for housebreaking a pup.

A wire kennel can such as this one often prove invaluable. At first, when you bring the puppy home, you can use a large kennel for many things. The wire kennel (measuring 30x18x20 inches or 76.2x45.72x50.8 cm) is perfect for sleeping quarters for the puppy, a place for the puppy to hang out when you are at work or running errands, a great place to housebreak the puppy, and generally a safe and secure space for your dog from puppy stages to adulthood.

First, notice the removable tray at the bottom of this crate. When you are housebreaking the pup, you can place a puppy pad in this tray. (Be forewarned – many puppies will shred the puppy pads, then they may have an accident. The tray allows you to pull out the mess, clean the tray, then put it back under the crate with ease.) This may be one of the chief reasons that I promote the use of a wire kennel as opposed to a bigger version of the travel crate. Clean-up of a plastic crate is much more involved.

Next, you want the puppy to believe the crate is a place of his own. So, you want to make the puppy feel comfortable inside the crate. One feature of this crate that I believe adds to the comfort of the pup is the fact that the wire allows the puppy to see that his family is still around rather than shutting him in the plastic crate which cuts off much of the pup's sight. Bonus points if you will leave the television on (or something with speaking voices, such as the radio; this gives the dog the impression that you are still home and helps with separation anxiety). Place the puppy's bed or blanket inside the crate. Leave a few toys inside as well. This will help to build that sense of the pup's ownership of the place.

Place a puppy pad in the tray under the crate. Again, some dogs will dig and shred the puppy pad. This can be aggravating at times, but, if you are patient, the puppy will grow out of this. It might help to tape the puppy pad down to the removable tray.

As the puppy ages and views the crate as his "space," the puppy will no longer relieve him or herself inside the crate. You can begin to move the puppy pad from a removable tray to a space beside the kennel. As the puppy uses the pad in that area, slowly move it to a door where you will be taking the dog out to have potty time. Eventually, the puppy will learn to go to the door when he needs to go out. Don't expect this to happen overnight, but, when Fido does begin to understand that this signals you his need to go out, he will continue the behavior.

Yes, you may also allow the puppy to sleep in the crate. In many ways, this is better for the puppy than sleeping with you. Plus, the crate provides a feeling of security. When puppies are very small, there is a tendency to want to keep them in bed with you. Unless you are prepared to keep the puppy in bed for the next fifteen years, then you should never start the habit. Small puppies may also have an accident in your bed if they cannot wake you to take them to the puppy pad at night, and, if a puppy as small as the Cavachon falls from the bed, he can be severely injured. Therefore, it's just a good idea not to bring the Cavachon puppy into bed with you from the very beginning. He will become acclimated to his crate, and he will soon see it as his "space."

Grooming supplies are also something you'll need in order to care for the Cavachon properly. Personally, I recommend taking the Cavachon for professional grooming appointments every eight to twelve weeks. In between, however, you can still perform touch-ups. You'll need a pin brush for daily brushing. You will also need a wide-tooth comb for after the bath. Some pet parents like to keep nail clippers. We can speak about grooming later, but some individuals would much rather the groomer or the vet take care of this chore. However, you may want to include this item in your list of must-haves just in case you need it.

Cavachon Dog Food – What is the Best Kind of Food for my Dog?

The Cavachon is typically a healthy dog; however, without a proper diet, the Cavachon can become malnourished. There are many options for providing the Cavachon with a proper diet, and you can even consider making home-cooked meals for your fur baby! The Cavachon may suffer from certain nutritional deficiencies which can make him feel lethargic at best and may detrimentally affect his overall health at worst. The Cavachon may often need more Vitamin A, magnesium, iron, Vitamin E, and calcium in order to be healthy.

Your Cavachon will need between 329 and 547 calories per day. While this number is sometimes difficult to determine when using dry dog food, you can use a half-cup and cup measurements to make sure that you are feeding the Cavachon enough. When feeding dry dog food, one cup in the morning and one at the evening feeding typically ensures that the Cavachon takes in the proper amount of calories each day. For dogs weighing between fifteen and twenty pounds, you may want to increase this by one half-cup at each feeding.

Speaking of dry dog food, how do I know that a particular dry dog food is a high-quality one? Do I *have* to purchase my dog's food at the veterinarian's office? No. All you need to do is familiarize yourself with the ingredients that make a dry food high quality, and ingredients that are simply fillers with no nutritional value.

You may think that you need to pay an arm and a leg to ensure you're getting high-quality food. This is not necessarily true. However, most very cheap dog foods are made with ingredients that are not very healthy. Turn to your list of ingredients on the dog food packaging. Two words to look for immediately are "by-product" and "corn syrup." Certainly, you're aware that corn syrup is the same as high fructose corn syrup in human food, and you are aware of the dangers of that food product. Consider it just as harmful to your dog as it is to you and your family. Corn syrup is a sweetener, and it will only cause weight gain. Corn syrup also has a more sinister side effect for dogs. Many dogs suffer from allergies, and one manifestation of these allergies is hair loss, a rash, or a never-ending itch. The Cavachon does not typically suffer from allergies, but, just as any human can develop an allergy, so can a Cavachon. Therefore, it is best to avoid dry dog food that contains corn syrup.

Let's talk about "by-product" ingredients. These are the cheap fillers that were mentioned earlier. Typically, you'll see the words chicken, beef, or fish in front of the "by-product." Sadly, this is basically the leftover parts that food manufacturers can do nothing else with. This may be internal organs, the intestines, but it can also contain damaged or diseased tissue, tumors, and ground bone. This may also be listed as bone meal by-product.

These are not animal muscles, which would be acceptable dry dog food. Be especially concerned if a by-product is one of the first ingredients listed; that means the by-product is one of the chief ingredients. It also means your dog will be getting very little nutrition at all from the dog food.

Now, let's get into more specifics of ingredients. First, we will discuss additives which can prove very harmful to your dog. Glyceryl Monostearate is a thickening agent. It contains a very dangerous chemical known as BHT. BHT stands for Butylated Hydroxytoluene, which is a preservative. Glyceryl Monostearate is one of the most commonly used additives in the food industry, but it is a chemical that is often unstable, and, therefore, unhealthy.

Phosphoric Acid is another chemical additive to look for and steer away from should you find it in a list of ingredients. This particular chemical is used in fertilizers and detergents. It's definitely not safe as a food product. Experts state that it is harmless, but your goal is to stay away from additives as much as possible.

Propylene Glycol is another chemical that is added to dry dog food so that it will not dry out. This chemical can also be found in anti-freeze and in other automotive fluids. Although it is supposed to be safe, consumed in high amounts, this additive can be harmful.

You likely know someone who can't eat gluten, and, if you do, you know that they have digestive issues. The same can be said for gluten in dog food. Corn gluten can cause allergic reactions as described above – the hair loss, itching, and the presence of whelps on your dog's skin. You may also see this as "corn gluten meal." Wheat gluten is similar to corn gluten; this product is created when the grain is "washed" in a method to remove the starch of the product. Once this process has been finished, there is little nutritional value in the remaining binder of wheat gluten. Again, gluten – wheat or corn variety – can cause allergic reactions in dogs. Even if this ingredient merely causes discomfort in your dog, you still want to avoid it.

Brewer's rice is another ingredient to avoid. Brewer's rice is the remnants of milled rice. Much of the product is simply a filler that has little nutritional value. Look for whole-grain rice as an ingredient instead.

Cereal Food fines are another by-product food additive. Literally, cereal food fines are the remnants of breakfast cereal. It's important to note that cereal food fines are of an unknown source, and they may contain any number of unknown sweeteners, chemical additives, and other chemicals. These are highly unhealthy for your dog.

Feeding Oatmeal is another food by-product and is generally what remains once whole oats have been processed. These are usually fillers and have little nutritional value. Soluble grain fermentation is another of these food by-products. These by-products are the result of human food and beverage production. While these fillers may not be harmful to your dog, they provide very little nutrition to your fur baby.

It should be evident with so many of these ingredients possessing little nutritional value that feeding them to your Cavachon might not harm the dog with harmful chemicals but can cause malnutrition. Remember that there are certain vitamins and minerals that the Cavachon tends to need more so than others. Feeding Fido a dry food with fillers and additives might keep him from being hungry, but Fido will suffer in other ways without proper nutrients.

Continuing with additives, here's another one that we know we should not eat as humans. Maltodextrin is a food additive that is a derivative of malted barley. Fermentation solubles are another barley by-product. Neither of these has much in the way of nutritional value, and they are better utilized to feed livestock rather than a dog.

Potato product is not a harmful additive, but more of a non-nutritional filler that is used in cheaply made dog food.

Soy flour is the result of the process where oil is removed from the soybean using a mechanical or solvent process. Not only is most of the nutritional value of the soybean removed when this process is completed, but the resulting flour may have hulls and other particles of the bean (which aren't usually edible prior to the process) in the flour product.

I want to really speak about the dangers of coloring agents in dry dog food. There is no need for any dog food to have a color. If you see Blue 2, Red 40, Yellow 5, Yellow 6, or Titanium Dioxide in the list of ingredients, put that food back on the shelf and look for something without food coloring additives. Dogs are attracted to food by smell, not by color. In addition, the chemicals in food colors can be very harmful to the dog. Blue 2 has been linked to brain tumors in lab mice, although the FDA has said that there was no definitive link and deemed Blue 2 safe for consumption. You'd do well to stay away from this food color, however.

Red 40 has not been definitively linked to cancer or other diseases in lab tests, but just because lab tests have been conflicting does not mean that Red 40 can't be harmful. Most often, you'll see Red 40 in human junk food, and we humans know what junk food does to our bodies.

Titanium oxide is an opaque powder that is used to "condition" dough. Although it is not known to be harmful to humans or animals, any and all food coloring additives should be avoided.

Yellow 5 and Yellow 6 are both highly controversial food coloring additives. Yellow 6 is the third most commonly added food color, and Yellow 5 is the second (most common food color additive). Yellow 5 has been shown to provoke allergic reactions in humans, although they are typically not the type associated with anaphylactic shock. If Yellow 5 causes mild allergic reactions in humans, you can reasonably expect the same in a dog. You might notice the Cavachon scratching more or gnawing at itchy spots, or you may observe the Cavachon losing hair. This is typically how an allergic reaction manifests itself in a dog.

Yellow 6 show that has been linked to cancerous tumors in animals, particularly in the adrenal gland and the kidney. The FDA continues to approve the use of the product, however, because they claim there is no link to human cancer. Again, avoid any food color additives. Dogs cannot tell what color their food is, and they will not eat food based on whether its attractive or not to the eye.

You may also find listed in the ingredients a few things that might seem healthy as they are derived from animals or plants: beef tallow, lard, poultry fat, and vegetable oil. These are also derivatives, and they have no nutritional value or very little value. While they might not cause allergic reactions, they are not good for the heart. It's best to avoid ingredients that provide little nutrition and may contribute to your dog's obesity (these fatty ingredients can cause your dog to gain weight while still lacking vital nutrients).

One final word to the wise, any time you see preservatives such as BHT, BHA, ethoxyquin, and the word "meal" in the ingredient list, avoid that dog food. There are many nutritious dog foods out there at a reasonable price. Furthermore, it's best to provide your dog with food that promotes her health and spend a little extra money monthly to feed your high-quality dog food. You'll save on veterinarian bills in the long run.

Dry dog food is not the only choice you have to feed your Cavachon. There are lots of great, high-quality wet (canned) foods on the market. Use the same criteria to screen the ingredients of a canned food product. You won't find the fillers and many of the preservatives in canned dog food as you will in dry dog food, but you may find that the meat used in the canned food is not of the quality you desire. When choosing canned food for your dog, look for certain phrases on the label. If you see the phrase "Made in the USA," then the regulations demand that the ingredients be made in the United States. Also, look for an AAPCO approved food. These phrases assure the consumer that the product meets certain nutritional standards.

There are those who cook for their dogs. What better way to ensure that Fido has all the vitamins and nutrients he needs by preparing his food yourself? (NOTE: An alternative to this is to supplement a prepared, homecooked meal with high-quality dry dog food. That way you know Fido is getting all the nutrients he needs, and his caloric needs are being met.) If you decide to prepare your dog's meals, you'll need sweet potatoes, green leafy vegetables (spinach is always a good idea as it cooks down easily), beans, and a protein source. Some add legumes as well. Boil the potatoes and mash them. Boil the spinach (or another equally nutritious leafy green veggie), and mix that into the potatoes. I prefer green beans when adding this part of the meal together. Typically, I do not use legumes, but I will use whole grain rice to replace the potatoes. As to the protein source, you can boil beef tips, chicken, lamb, or fish. Mix in a teaspoon of oil (you can use olive oil, flaxseed oil, or fish oil). This is good for the dog's joints. Again, about a cup to a cup and one-half of food at each meal is plenty for the Cavachon.

One word of advice: you might want to add a vitamin supplement if you go the home-prepared route. Make sure this supplement includes a digestive enzyme.

There are those who put their pet on a "raw food" diet. The raw food diet mirrors the wild diet that your dog's ancestors once took in – bones, grass, small prey. The issue that many veterinarians are seeing is infections in the joints associated with eating raw meat. Many opponents are concerned with the consumption of raw bones, as they do not often digest well. There are commercially made raw food offerings; however, many of them are not of high quality. If you do decide to use this approach to feeding your Cavachon, do a great deal of research before you go fully into the raw food diet. It is especially not appropriate for young puppies.

Cavachon Dog Beds

When searching for the perfect Cavachon bed, be sure to keep in mind your dog's relatively small size, and proportion the bed to fit the dog. If you set Fido up in a bed that's too big for him, you're setting him up for feelings of insecurity. Look for a bed that's just roomy enough for your dog to stretch out into a sleeping position. Smaller dogs like the Cavachon are much more likely to get cold, so it's important to find a bed that will provide her with warmth. Keep in mind that the Cavachon DOES have medium-length to long hair, so you may want to steer away from the covered beds, instead offering a blanket for extra warmth.

Nest dog beds are the covered dog beds, and they a popular choice for small dogs. Generally, they're round or oval with padding and raised sides (or a completely covered top) to help your Cavachon feel secure and comfortable. A word of caution – make sure the filling materials are of good quality so that your dog will be protected from hard floor surfaces.

A concern when shopping for bedding for smaller breeds is the dog's need to stay warm. Simple padded beds often do not keep a small dog feeling secure and warm. However, with the Cavachon, if you allow your dog's hair to grow out, then you may not need a nesting or slumber bed.

Consider a bed that allows for burrowing. You may start out your puppy with a regular bed and a blanket. Notice how they treat the blanket. Do they try to get under the blanket? Then you can try a nesting bed or a slumber bed. Dogs can fall restfully into the softer cushioning of the bed, feeling as if they are burying themselves, and garnering more security and a sense of safety in these beds.

Is it possible that your Cavachon has allergies? Finding a bed for the Cavachon with allergies may be a chore because you'll have to find a bed with cushioning that does not contain any allergy triggers. Cedar is often a trigger for allergies, and it is fairly common in dog bedding, and on the outer cover of beds. If you find your Cavachon experiencing skin irritation, and you're sure that it is not due to food, then try a dog bed cover. There are hypoallergenic covers available at your local pet supply store. In addition, a bed cover can help prevent dust mites; you can also remove it to wash and regularly clean, which will also promote fewer allergic triggers.

Cavachon Puppy Care – Taking Care of a Young Cavachon Pup

After you finish puppy-proofing (see chapter six), you'll need to take the puppy to the vet for a check-up. Bring the puppy's shot record so that no immunizations are duplicated. For the first four months of the puppy's life, you'll need to bring him in for booster shots.

Decide where the puppy will sleep. Yes, we've discussed this before, and the best place is likely the kennel. Make the kennel seem like a home away from home. Soon, the pup will feel that the kennel is "his" space, and you may notice that he ventures into the kennel for naps quite often.

Feeding a puppy is a little different from feeding an adult dog. A puppy may need only a quarter of what an adult dog needs in the way of food. Start small (one-quarter cup) twice daily. You can supplement this with a little canned food (about half of a small can per feeding). You can also introduce treats, but you should save these for training and for rewards.

Make sure that water is constantly available. Also, make sure that the puppy knows where her water is. When you first bring her home, make sure that you take her to the watering bowl after naps and after a meal. She will learn in no time where everything is set up.

CHAPTER 6

Living with the Cavachon – What Can You Expect?

T he great thing about the Cavachon is that they are generally very happy dogs, and they typically add to the lives of the families who give them forever homes. They are intelligent dogs who are easily trained, and they adapt to many different living situations.

The Cavachon will accompany his family just about anywhere!

Cavachon Puppies – How Can You Prepare Your Home for Them?

To a young puppy, your home is a playground full of areas to explore. This often takes place as the puppy chews, licks, and climbs onto various areas where he has no business being. Protect the Cavachon puppy while saving your furniture and shoes by puppy-proofing your home, or at least puppy-proof the areas in which the puppy will be frequenting.

Treat puppy-proofing like you would baby-proofing a home. Pick up anything that you think would be chewable, especially if it is small enough to be swallowed. For your own peace of mind, rig a system of where you'll store shoes so that the puppy cannot get to them and chew them. A puppy whose teeth are coming in will destroy a pair of shoes in no time! Make sure that any cables – especially electrical wires, are covered, and stored away from access to the puppy. Put the wires under or behind furniture. At the same time, use puppy gates to corral the puppy into areas where, should she have a potty accident, it will not damage your flooring.

You also want to make sure that you have removed any items that might end up being poisonous to your new dog. As a general rule, I recommend removing plants of any kind up and away from a curious puppy. There are some plants that are definitely toxic to dogs, but they are also prone to playing and turning things over. Therefore, keep plants away from a young puppy. Cleaning products should be kept up and away from a puppy. You may even have to keep them on a higher cabinet shelf. Some pups are smart enough to open a cabinet door (you can prevent this by getting child safety locks for cabinets). Grapes, chocolate, and onions must also be kept away from dogs at any age as all are toxic to canines.

When you think the job's done, get down to the floor level and check things out from a puppy's point of view. Be particular about checking under the sofa and in the floor-level places you don't usually pay much attention to. This might seem a little much, but it is a great way to make sure you didn't miss anything that's attractive to your pup.

Cavachon Food

In Chapter Five, we discussed what a healthy diet for a Cavachon should include. Many of these decisions are personal preferences. I prefer dry food with some wet food supplementing it. I sometimes also boil chicken or beef tips and mix in with the dry dog food. Occasionally, I will boil rice and add in as well. This is just to vary their diet from time to time. Keep in mind that some dogs get used to dry food, and when you introduce wet or canned food, they may experience an upset stomach. However, allow them to have canned food in small portions with their dry food, and upset stomach is often avoided.

Keep in mind the advice concerning food ingredients given in chapter five. Look for organic-based commercial dog food, and read the ingredient list. Avoid those with harmful additives, food dyes, and fillers.

*With a proper diet, the Cavachon will be happy
and healthy for the better part of two decades.*

Do Cavachons Shed? Are they considered hypoallergenic?

The Cavachon is considered to be a low-shedding dog. The designer breed IS considered to be hypoallergenic; however, one must keep in mind that all dogs shed. Some shed very little, but they DO shed. The Cavachon does not shed much, and the breed does not produce a lot of dander (skin flakes) that often provoke an allergic reaction in a person. So, yes, the Cavachon is considered hypoallergenic, but the breed will shed at least twice a year.

Do Cavachons Molt?

The term "molt" means the same thing as shed. So, yes, the Cavachon does molt. However, if you will brush the Cavachon with a pin brush once a day, you will see very little shedding from the Cavachon.

What are the Typical Cavachon Exercise Requirements?

The Cavachon is a boisterous breed that loves playtime, but the designer dog is not considered hyperactive. A daily walk of at least one half-hour is usually just enough to meet the exercise requirements of this breed. Keep in mind that the Cavachon also enjoys indoor playtime. Remember those toys we discussed previously? Grab a ball and play fetch in the hallway. No time to play interactively? Fill a food puzzle toy with a little peanut butter, and let Fido go crazy trying to get to every nibble. When the weather is inclement, and you are tied up with chores or work, a toy such as the food puzzle toy will keep your puppy from becoming bored and getting into mischief.

What is the Average Size of the Cavachon?

The typical Cavachon is about twelve inches tall at the shoulder and weighs approximately ten pounds. Depending on the size of the parents, however, the Cavachon you bring home may be larger when fully grown – upwards of eighteen pounds and thirteen inches in height, which is the upper range of height and weight for both the Bichon Frise and the Cavalier King Charles Spaniel parent breeds. Note: If you get a Cavachon that is an F2 (second-generation) offspring, then you will need to look at the Cavachon parents themselves in order to estimate the size of your own Cavachon pup.

Cavachon Dogs – What will Grooming Be Like? What Are Some Hairstyles for this Breed?

Unless you have experience grooming a dog, the best advice I can give you is to ask your vet for the recommendation of a good groomer (if you're lucky, your vet just might employ a groomer on his or her staff). Allow the groomer to take care of the major haircuts. You can maintain the coat in-between visits to the groomer. You can also bathe your Cavachon at home; you do not need to carry him to the groomer for this.

Some experts recommend using one a metal comb with wide teeth. Most state that the wide-tooth metal comb works through the hair, and takes out any tangles that might occur. About a week after the initial trip to the groomer's, about the time when the hair starts growing again, your Cavachon will start getting tangles, and you will have to comb him at least three times a week. The frequency of combing will increase as your Cavachon's hair grows longer; so you will want to comb it every other day. Combing can take between a half-hour to an hour, but, remember, the more often you comb your Cavachon, the fewer tangles you will have to comb out.

Experts recommend that you begin grooming your Cavachon when the puppy is young. If you get the pup used to grooming, nail clipping and cleaning his ears at an early age, then the dog will be accustomed to the routine, and will not fuss or misbehave.

You might be able to get away with bathing the Cavachon every two to three weeks, especially during the cooler months. Again, you can bathe the Cavachon any time you wish; you do not need to take Fido to the groomer for this. But, keep in mind that you need to choose an all-natural shampoo for this.

Choosing the right shampoo for your Cavachon is so important. You should choose a shampoo that contains as many natural ingredients as possible. However, don't be fooled by a shampoo that is blue and smells like berries – that's not an all-natural shampoo. It doesn't matter what is on the label; many shampoos claim to be "organic" or "all-natural," but they still contain some chemicals. For some reason, manufacturers can get away with using these labels, although they are not accurate. An all-natural shampoo that is truly natural or organic will generally have very little smell, will be a pale yellow color, and will not suds up when you lather your pup. That blue color mentioned previously? That's typically a chemical additive that can wreak havoc on your Cavachon's skin. All-natural shampoos do not create much of a lather; lather is the product of sulfates that can also harm a dog's skin. Scents in organic shampoos are also very light. A fruity-scented smell is a sure sign of chemical additives.

Here are some things to look for on the list of ingredients and AVOID as they are very harmful to a dog's skin.

- Added dyes or colorants
- Examples are D&C Blue No. 4, or D&C Yellow No. 8, CI 1940 (also called Tartrazine, which is strongly linked to allergic reactions, migraines, hyperactivity, and even tumors).
- Added fragrance or perfumes derived from chemicals
- Parabens - look instead for shampoos that use citrus seed extracts, and natural vitamins A, C, and E.
- Mineral oil
- Stearalkonium chloride
- Sodium laureth sulfate and sodium laurel
- DEA, cocamide DEA and lauramide DEA

A close-cut grooming style is a great summer cut for the Cavachon.

Another summer cut for the Cavachon. Slightly longer yet still cooler than a natural coat.

A slightly shaggy cut.

Longer Hair Style of the Cavachon.

Growth Chart – Miniature Cavachon Puppies, Teacup Cavachon, Cavachon Full Grown (Cavachon Weight Chart)

Teacup Cavachon	Very small, 8 - 10 pounds (3.63 kg - 4.54 kg)
Miniature Cavachon	Small, 11 - 13 pounds (4.99 - 5.9 kg)
Full Grown Cavachon	Average, 15 - 18 pounds (6.80 - 8.16 kg)

Do Cavachons have Allergies?

Yes and no. Most Cavachons do not have allergies, but some are prone to them. This is not necessarily due to any genetic factor in the Cavachon. Some Cavachons might have allergies to certain food products (which is why it's so important to ensure you are avoiding those ingredients discussed previously). Often, this is a trial and error situation. With dogs, the chief symptoms of an allergy are skin irritation, redness, whelps, constant itching, and hair loss. You will need to take your dog to the veterinarian so that you can begin eliminating what might be causing the allergic reactions. The veterinarian will ask about the dog's diet. If you have been feeding the dog a diet full of nutrients and free of the meal and animal by-products that could cause allergies, then you can likely eliminate the idea that food might be causing the allergy. Next, consider the grooming products you are using. As long as you are using the natural shampoos that do not contain harsh chemicals, your Cavachon should not be having an allergic reaction to it. If the Cavachon is still having allergic reactions, and you have eliminated the food or product allergy factor, then you may have an issue with fleas and a flea allergy. This is where your veterinarian will come in handy. He or she can help you to safely eliminate the fleas and rid your pup of the allergies that are making him miserable.

What are Some Other Cavachon Health Issues?

Although the Cavachon is a typically healthy dog, they may experience some problems which are genetically inherited from the Bichon Frise parent breed or the Cavalier King Charles Spaniel parent breed. These problems may include hip dysplasia, heart murmur, congestive heart failure, ear infections, eye problems, liver problems, and certain autoimmune diseases. Although many purebred dog breeders will test their breeding stock for genetic diseases, some designer dog breeders may not. You can inquire about the parents of your prospective pup and their health history. This can help you to ensure that you are getting the healthiest pup available.

Why Do Some Cavachons Tend to Have Eye Stains? Do Cavachons Tend to Have Eye Health Problems?

Excessive tearing in canines is a condition called epiphora. A dog's eye reacts to irritations by making tears. Some breeds have more sensitive eyes than others, and the Cavachon Is one of them. This Is a genetic issue as both the Bichon Frise and the Cavalier King Charles Spaniel are genetically prone to this condition.

In most dogs, the tear ducts allow excess tears to dissolve naturally. The Cavachon and its parent breeds often suffer from clogged ducts or hair around the eye that can cause the tears to spill out of the eye and stain the white fur around the eye socket. Most of the common causes of tear stains In Cavachons are as follows:

- Shallow eye sockets
- Eyelids turned inwards
- Hair around the eye
- Blocked tear ducts

How Do I Prevent Health Problems in the Cavachon?

First, make sure that your Cavachon receives healthy food. Next, take him or her in for regular veterinarian checks. Groom her regularly. Watch for any skin irritation, and get that under control quickly. You won't be able to prevent all Cavachon health issues, but these steps will go a long way in promoting good health in your Cavachon.

CHAPTER 7

Cavachon Puppies and Cavachon Adults for Sale – How Can You Find The Right Dog at the Right Price?

W e have discussed finding a good breeder. The future health of your Cavachon pup is dependent upon a reputable breeder who did everything possible to make sure that the puppies he or she brought into the world are not only healthy when they come to you, the new pet parent, but also for years to come. Previously, we discussed prices for the Cavachon pup. It can range greatly depending on your location, the necessity of shipping a dog from a breeder far away, and the level of experience of the breeder (hobbyists might not charge as much as a breeder by trade).

A brown Cavachon puppy.

Cavachon Dogs – What is the average price of this hybrid dog?

As of this writing, the average price for a Cavachon is $847.00.

Are you seeking a puppy with a superior lineage? Trying to determine how much a puppy with breeding rights and papers would cost? You should expect to pay a premium price for a puppy advertised as show quality. You should plan anywhere from $1,600 or even more for a Cavachon with prestigious breeding lines. The average cost for all Cavachons sold is $800, but prices near $2,000 are not uncommon either.

🐕 86

How Do I Find a Cavachon puppy or adult dog near me?

While you can do a simple internet search to find a breeder near you, it is best to really research breeders before you buy a puppy from them sight unseen. Follow the advice in the previous chapter. Set up a phone interview, then narrow down to three breeders you feel are ethical. Plan a visit, and meet the breeder and the mom (and hopefully your potential pup!). Don't forget that there is a list of reputable breeders in the bonus chapter.

You can also rely on word of mouth when looking for a reputable breeder. Although this method of making sure that a breeder is an ethical one, it is just the first of many ways that you can verify whether a breeder is really what his or her website claims to be. Do network, and do speak to those with knowledge of breeders in your area.

CHAPTER 8

Cavachon Mixes and Colors – What are the Different Mixed Breeds and Cavachon Color Patterns that Exist?

I f you'll look at the grooming styles in chapter six, you will see just how varied the Cavachon looks. Some are black and white. Some are Blenheim. Some may be almost all white. Even if you can meet both of your potential pup's parents, you still won't be able to tell definitively what a Cavachon pup will look like. In this chapter, we'll explore some of the different coat colors and patterns.

The adorable black Cavachon would be a great addition to your home.

Cavachon Dog – Compare the Cavapoo and the Cavachon – Which is Better?

Most Cavachons have thick, fluffy coats that can are either curly or wavy. They have adorable faces with large brown eyes, which adds to their appeal.

Their coats are often soft and rather long. They come in a variety of colors which includes white with black, apricot or tan markings; brown; red; tricolor; and white.

Cavapoos are also small dogs, but they tend to be slightly taller than the Cavachons. They usually weigh around seventeen to twenty-two pounds (eight to ten kg), which means they are also a little heavier when compared to the Cavachon. Cavapoos often tend to look more like one parent breed than the other. Some end up looking more like Poodles while other Cavapoos favor the Cavalier King Charles Spaniel parent breed; their coat texture is similar. The most common coat colors seen in Cavapoos are black, white, chestnut, gold, Blenheim (chestnut and white), and tricolor (black, white, and tan).

Cavachons are known for being affectionate dogs; they are social and love their "people." They love spending as much time as possible with their families. They are typically easy-going dogs, and they enjoy other animals as long as they are raised together.

Cavachons are also known as a perfect "first dog" for inexperienced owners. A Cavachon tends to greet everyone they meet. Because they form such strong bonds with their families, they never like to be left alone for long; they are happier with families where at least one member stays home during the day. Otherwise, they are prone to experiencing separation anxiety. When they do, they may become destructive or otherwise act out.

Similarly, the Cavapoo is easy going and does not enjoy being alone for very long. They are also highly adaptable, which means they are just as happy living in an apartment or in a larger home. Cavapoos are a wonderful choice for first-time dog owners also because they are so adaptable and willing to please their owners.

Cavapoos are intelligent dogs that need to be provided plenty of mental and physical activity (often, mental stimulation is as important or more important than physical movement). Because they wish to please their humans, train them with a reward system rather than punishing them or using harsh corrective measures.

Cavachons shed throughout the year, but more during the spring and the fall just as other dogs do. However, they are considered to be "low-shedders."

Cavapoos shed steadily throughout the year, but less so than the Cavachon. They shed the most during the spring and the fall when their coats begin to change texture for the upcoming seasons.

The Cavachon is highly intelligent, as is the Cavapoo. Each of them tends to be somewhat mischievous. Although they are willing to please their owners, they often learn bad habits as easily as they do positive ones. Remember to train each of these breeds by rewarding good behavior rather than disciplining them for bad behavior.

We have discussed the health issues that the Cavachon tends to experience; however, the possible health concerns of the Cavapoo are as follows: syringomyelia, mitral valve disease, cataracts, and hip dysplasia. They may also suffer from patellar luxation, PRA (progressive retinal atrophy), skin conditions, or epilepsy.

What is the result of breeding a Cavachon with a Shih Tzu (Cavachon x Shih Tzu)?

The result of this cross-breeding is a Cava Tzu. This small, adorable little dog is very smart. They are sociable, and they tend to get along with other dogs. They might not be good for families with small children as they can be frail.

Brown Cavachon

The Cavachon may be a wide variety of colors; one is brown. This is dependent upon the colors and genetics of the parents.

Sable Cavachon

The sable-colored Cavachon is often a light brown color all over its body, and there may be a slight "dusting" of black in certain areas of the coat.

Cavachon Poodle – Is the Cockapoo a Cavachon Cross? What is a Cavapoochon?

A Cavachon Poodle is the combination of a Cavachon and a Miniature Poodle. This would be the Cavapoochon. However, the *Cockapoo* designer dog is NOT a Cavachon cross, whereas the Cavapoochon is.

Red Cavachon

A red Cavachon will be a reddish-orange color all over.

Black Cavachon

A black Cavachon is black all over its body. This color is usually the result of two black Cavachons being paired together. (An F1 generation bred with another F1 generation.)

Tri-Color Cavachon

A tri-color Cavachon is typically brown, white, and tan.

What is the Cavanese or Cavanese Puppies? What is this versus a Cavachon? Is this the same as Havachon puppies?

A Cavanese is a cross between a Cavalier King Charles Spaniel and a Havanese. The Cavanese and the Cavachon only share one pet parent breed – the Cavalier King Charles Spaniel. The Havanese is a small dog, but his colors and coat pattern is very different from the Bichon Frise parent breed of the Cavachon. So, while they are both small, they may have very different appearances due to their parentage. The Havachon is a cross between the Havanese and the Bichon Frise. It will have many of the same characteristics of a Cavachon and a Cavanese.

What is the difference between the Cavalier King Charles Spaniel and the Cavachon?

The Cavalier King Charles Spaniel is one of the parent breeds of the Cavachon. They share much of the same genetics, but the Cavachon will have wavy – or even curly hair compared to the Cavalier King Charles Spaniel.

What is a Cavamalt?

The Cavamalt is a cross between the Cavalier King Charles Spaniel and the Maltese. The Cavamalt will look much like the Cavachon, but her hair will be longer, silky, and straight.

What is the Cavachon Cross/Bichon Frise/ Cavachon Bichon Puppy?

These terms are simply other ways to describe the Cavachon, a cross of the Bichon Frise and the Cavalier King Charles Spaniel.

Golden Cavachon

The Golden Cavachon is a Cavachon that is golden or tan in color.

CHAPTER 9

Cavachon Training – What Should You Know?

Now that you've brought Baby home, you are ready to begin working on training. Wait – what? Yes, I said once the puppy is home, you need to begin training him so that he understands your routine. This does not mean that you will be training your Cavachon for a dog show or even teaching him tricks. Rather, you will show him where he sleeps, where he eats, and how he is expected to behave. Although he will pick up on where to eat and sleep fairly quickly or easily, showing him how to behave will be the training that takes the first year or two of his life to complete.

Your Cavachon will enjoy playing with you!

What are the Things you Need for Cavachon Training?

You'll want to have plenty of treats, a leash, a collar or harness, at the very least. You may need to add to this depending on what you are training for. If you are housebreaking, you'll also need puppy pads.

Time is often the most important commodity you'll need for training your Cavachon. Dogs learn best by repetition. If you're housebreaking the Cavachon, you will want to develop a routine and stick to it as best as possible.

How Do I Crate or Kennel Train my Cavachon?

In chapter five, we discussed what to place in the kennel in order to welcome your puppy home. When your puppy is small, you can simply place him in the kennel. If your dog is a little older when you begin training, you can coax him into the kennel by putting a trail of treats leading into the structure. When you are training the puppy, begin by leaving the dog only for short periods of time. (Note: When you are training the Cavachon puppy to sleep in the crate, you will leave them in overnight. This advice is for the daytime. You don't want the puppy to feel that he is locked up all the time.) When you put him in the kennel, walk out of his sight for about ten minutes. Do leave a television on, or maybe the radio. Come back, and act as if you haven't seen the puppy in a very long time. The puppy will learn that you might have to go away for a bit, but you WILL come back to him soon. Only do this four or five times per day until the puppy gets used to the crate as "his" space.

A word of wisdom – never lock the puppy in the crate as a punishment. You'll never get him trained if you do.

Cavachon Training Tips – What Skills Must it Learn?

Your Cavachon needs to be socialized. Get her around other people, especially responsible children. Let her be around someone who might have a loud voice and boisterous personality.

Let her be around men wearing hats (some dogs are never around this, and they will bark and get scared even if someone they know is wearing a hat). Allow the Cavachon to be around other dogs (supervised, of course). Bring in a friend with a friendly cat. Expose the Cavachon to other people and animals, and she will never be scared or not know how to act in new situations. You'll want the Cavachon to know how to walk along with you, and you'll want the Cavachon to know some obedience commands.

Social skills come naturally to the Cavachon, so taking the time to expose your pup to different people and other animals is a fairly easy way to help them acquire the behavioral skills you desire. With obedience, you will want them to learn some general obedience commands. Typically, these commands include sit, stay, heel, and, of course, the word "no."

You'll have more success with training if you wait until your Cavachon is mature enough to start true training. Feel free to introduce the Cavachon pup of ten weeks or older to the command words, but you may see that Fido is not ready to start actual training for a month or eight weeks more. Start with treats and the basics. "Sit" is one of the easiest commands. Be sure your dog is in a standing position. Get his attention and show him a treat. Put the treat at his nose level, but do not allow him to take the treat. Instead, slowly raise the treat so that Fido's nose follows it. You'll notice that your dog's rear is naturally headed for the floor as he raises his head to follow the treat. As he does this, say, "Sit." When he gets to that seated position, praise him, and give the treat. Repeat a few more times, then take a break. Remember that, with puppies, it is important to repeat on a daily basis rather than attempting to learn a command all in one day.

Most of the other commands are for a dog that is a little more mature and is already leash-trained.

Speaking of leash-training, it is very important that you get Fido accustomed to walking beside you while on a leash. You should never allow your puppy to be on the ground before she has had all her vaccinations. This ensures that she does not contract Parvo, or the Parvovirus, which is an infection that can live on the ground through even freezing weather and persistent heatwaves. Parvo can be deadly, and it often comes on so quickly that a puppy may be near death before symptoms point to the virus. However, you can work on leash-training at home, indoors. Your puppy will likely want to walk alongside you, so simply attach the leash to her collar and let her follow along. One she is accustomed to the leash, then you can begin teaching her to heel.

To teach your Cavachon to heel, you'll first need to show your puppy what the "heel" position is. Start in a room that has no distractions – no children who wish to play, no toys, no noise that might catch your pup's attention. Some experts say you need not even start with the leash attached. First, get your dog's attention and say, "Watch me." When the dog does this, offer a treat. It's important that your dog watch you in order to know how to follow your cues. Repeat this a few times until the dog will do as you ask when you give the command to watch.

Next, work on the pup's following your lead take a step or two. If she follows at your side, then give her a treat. Increase this by a couple of steps each time you work on this part of heeling. Each time she keeps up at your side, give her a treat. Repeat this until she will watch and wait for you, then follow along with her head close to your led.

Now you'll want to add stop to this. This is the time you'll want to add the leash if you have not already. When you stop, and the dog continues ahead of you, gently tug on the leash, then put yourself physically in front of her. Say "stop." You will have to repeat this a few times so that your pup understands that she is not to walk ahead of you. Work up to a point where you are able to get the dog to stop when you stop walking.

Some dogs also tend to lag when walking on the leash. Get your dog to walk alongside you, then allow her to lag behind. Now, say, "watch me." When the dog comes to you, say "heel." Walk a few steps, repeating the command. Reward the puppy with a treat and praise for walking alongside you; add a few steps each time you practice and repeat the reward.

Teaching your Cavachon to stay is another simple command that most dogs should know. With a puppy, you may only be able to achieve the "stay" position for a second or two, but, reward her anyway, as you can use this to build on longer "stay" times. Have the dog sit. Reward this. Then, open your palm and begin to step backward while saying, "stay." If the dog gets up immediately from the sitting position to follow you, do not reward her. Simply put her back in the sitting position, and repeat the behavior until the dog will sit – even momentarily – when you begin to back away. Work on increasing the time that the pup stays in the sitting position, and reward her each time that she remains seated as you back away.

How Do I Deal with Negative Cavachon Behavior?

The best way to deal with bad behavior is to use gentle correction. Even better, you should make a point to reward good behavior so that the puppy is encouraged to "be good" rather than continue with negative behavior. This is especially true when you are working on training. It's always a good idea to teach the Cavachon pup, "no."

Often dog owners find themselves telling a puppy "no" *after* a negative behavior has occurred. This is never the way to go about teaching a dog "no" or preventing negative behavior from taking place. Instead, begin teaching the dog the word "no" just as you would any other command. Start by showing the puppy a treat in your hand, but do not let her have it. Instead, close your hand into a fist around the treat. Allow the puppy to smell your hand and maybe even lick it, but do not offer her the treat. Say "no," as you do this. Be sure to say "no" sternly, but no so sharply that the dog thinks she's being punished for something. Only offer the treat when the dog leaves your closed hand alone. You'll need to repeat this part of training many, many times, so don't be put off if you do.

CHAPTER 10

Should You Show
Your Cavachon?

This chapter discusses what it's like to be in a dog show with your Cavachon. You will want to obtain the services of a mentor to help. You will also want to begin training your Cavachon well before you ever enter the show ring. Many owners who show their Cavachons state that this activity helps to draw them even closer to their dogs. Certainly, training will help to bond you and your pup. However, the Cavachon is considered a crossbreed dog, so your opportunities to show him may seem somewhat limited. However, there are some dog show competitions that are meant just for hybrid dogs, and this might be just the event in which to enter your Cavachon.

The Cavachon is a bit of a show-off, why not teach him to be a show dog?

Getting a Feel for Dog Shows

Perhaps the first thing you'll want to do is begin attending shows. Take notice of what they require a dog to do. Join a few local clubs, and check out their guidelines. Begin showing the Cavachon at these local events so that they understand what it is you expect of them.

Although the American Kennel Club has traditionally closed its competition to mixed-breed dogs, as of 2013, they are incorporating many competitions that allow for the showing and competition of designer dogs such as the Cavachon. Check with local AKC-affiliated clubs in order to determine if you and your Cavachon can participate.

Perhaps your best opportunity for showing the Cavachon might be at a show sponsored by the Mixed Breed Dog Club of America. A competition sponsored by this club will not focus so much on conformation (the way it would at an AKC-sponsored event where the breed standards are a part of the competition) but more on what makes a dog a good dog. Dogs are judged on their overall physical condition, obedience, and temperament rather than a rigorous set of breed standards.

The Crufts dog show is a popular competition just for mixed breed or crossbreed dogs. It is held in the United Kingdom, and, in recent years, the original Crufts competition has expanded to the Scruffts competition. In order to compete in the Scruffts competition, the Cavachon will need to compete in qualification heats at various locations in the United Kingdom. Once your dog has qualified, then he will be invited to be a part of the annual competition.

Should I Show my Dog, or Should I Hire a Handler?

This is a completely a personal decision. If you have health issues that might prevent you from guiding your dog through the show routine, then you can hire a handler. However, many owners wish to work with and show their dog. Then again, if you have not had much experience training a dog, you may wish to put the handler in charge of both training and showing.

Show-specific Training

The training you provide your pup for the show ring will be different from the training you give him for being around the house. Of course, you will want the Cavachon to be able to act appropriately before, during, and after the actual competition. You'll want to make sure that the Cavachon is well-behaved among other dogs, and it is absolutely imperative that the Cavachon is not hyperactive and responds to your commands. You will want to make sure that your Cavachon knows how to heel, sit, and come before you enter him into a competition.

CHAPTER 11

The Cavachon Golden Years – How Can You Make Them the Best Years?

A senior Cavachon is one that has reached ten or so years of age. Many Cavachons this age are living just as fully as they did at a younger age. Still, there are a few issues that may make life difficult for an older dog.

Because the Cavachon is a smaller designer dog, chances are he will live a little longer than the average dog. If your Cavachon is healthy, then it may live for the better part of fourteen years (or longer!). Although many Cavachons are still quite active into their later years, you will likely notice that once your Cavachon reaches ten years of age, she will begin to slow down just a little and may sleep a little longer than previously was her habit. You might begin to notice that your Cavachon begins graying around her nose and eyes, and she may not run and jump as much as she once did. You may also notice her barking more often. She may not hear as well, and you may notice her eyesight beginning to falter. However, you can still make your Cavachon's older years just as happy as her early years.

Joint Pain

The Cavachon may experience some health issues that make them prone to arthritis and joint pain. You can help the senior dog by providing a nutritional supplement such as glucosamine and chondroitin, to strengthen your dog's joints. Although you might think your Cavachon should spend time resting in order to satisfy those achy joints, nothing could be further from the truth. In actuality, it's better for your Cavachon if you insist upon a minimum of exercise each day, even for only ten or fifteen minutes. The more you allow your Cavachon to lie around and sleep (given that she is otherwise healthy), the worse you are actually making the stiff joints associated with arthritis. Again, your veterinarian can provide you with a proper supplement regimen that will give your Cavachon some relief from swelling and joint pain associated with arthritis.

Sight or Hearing Problems

The older Cavachon may have some issues with losing his sight and/or hearing. If this occurs, you'll need to make some adjustments. You may begin to notice that your dog has an opaque spot in one or both eyes. This is a cataract, much like elderly humans develop. Some of these opaque spots stay fairly small. They may make the dog's vision blurry, but not completely block his vision. However, some cataracts become thicker over time, or they may grow in size (widen). If this becomes the case, you may need to seek treatment in order to prevent your dog's complete blindness. It is also important to note that sometimes the blue-gray cloudiness present in your dog's eye might not be a cataract, but a naturally occurring condition known as nuclear sclerosis. If this is the case, the vet will not likely recommend treatment.

Untreated cataracts may break free from the connective tissue holding it in place. If this happens, there's the possibility that the cataract can block fluid from naturally draining from the eye, and then glaucoma can set in. Even if this doesn't occur, the cataract can cause inflammation that may be quite painful to your dog. Therefore, it's best to treat any gray/blue color in your dog's eye as if it is a cataract and see your vet.

There is little you can do to treat hearing loss in your elderly Cavachon, and it is almost inevitable as your dog ages. Some individuals train their dogs to follow hand signals. Others may use more "non-traditional" signals as a means of communicating with the aging Cavachon. You'll need to make some adjustments in how you carry out your daily routine with your dog. When walking your Cavachon, you may need to keep your dog on a leash so that it does not venture away from you and into traffic or other dangerous situations. You'll also need to adjust your routine and behavior so that you don't startle your dog. If possible, refrain from rearranging furniture or making major changes in routine, as this can be quite upsetting for the elderly pooch who can no longer see or hear as well as he once could.

Exercise Requirements

This is another area that will change. You'll still want to keep up the half-hour of daily walking, but you'll likely need to break this up into shorter walks. You may also consider swimming, which is easier on the joints. Unless your vet instructs you otherwise, the longer you can keep your Cavachon active, the more quality of life she will have. Your walks may only be ten minutes or so at a time, and you may not be able to get your Cavachon to engage in fetch any longer, but you can adjust your Cavachon's exercise so that your dog is still active but not involved in anything that would put pressure on its joints.

Other Considerations

There can be other considerations when you are the parent of an elderly Cavachon. As the dog ages, it may not be able to control his bladder as well as before. If you notice that your dog can no longer go from a final walk at night until your usual time in the morning, then you might put puppy pads in his kennel so that he is protected in the event of an accident (this will also make clean-up easier for you).

Try not to leave an elderly Cavachon alone at home for long periods of time. When an elderly dog starts to lose his hearing and sight, more anxiety presents than before. Try to spend as much time with your dog as possible. It is imperative that the Cavachon have as much water as needed, and, if you notice your pooch drinking less and less progressively, you should see your vet to ensure there are no underlying health issues with your senior Cavachon.

When your Cavachon reaches the "golden years," it becomes more vulnerable to kidney disease and possible degenerative illnesses. Obesity is also another issue that many aging dogs have to face. Keeping your Cavachon at a healthy weight will help to promote a longer, healthier life for your dog. Each of these issues can be monitored with the help of your vet.

CHAPTER 12

Conclusion

T he Cavachon is a delightful little dog, and bringing home this particular designer dog to join your family will prove a reward to all of you, no doubt! I want to thank you for joining me on this journey of learning all the ins and outs of this unique breed. Don't forget about the bonus chapter – there are some helpful links listed there.

The Cavachon is known for its affectionate facial expressions.

The Cavachon is a happy, active designer dog.

The Cavachon is quite the charming little dog.

CHAPTER 13

Bonus Chapter – Your Trusted Cavachon Resource Guide

United States Breeder Resource List

- **Gleneden Cavachons**

  http://www.cavachon.com/id10.html

  This kennel claims to be the first to breed and promote the Cavachon designer dog.

- **Foxglove Cavachons**

  http://foxglovecavachonpuppies.com/

  This kennel is located in Ohio; they have thirty years of experience in breeding Cavachon and Cavapoo pups.

- **Cavachons by Design**

  https://www.cavachonsbydesign.com/

  This Tennessee-based breeder is a family-owned business.

- **Cavachons from the Monarchy**

  http://cavachonsfromthemonarchy.com/

  This breeder is located in Massachusetts.

- **Briarthorn Cavachon Puppies**

  http://www.briarthorndesignerpuppies.com/

  This family-owned breeder is located in Kent, Ohio.

United States Rescue/Cavachon Adoption Resource List

North Shore Animal League America

http://www.animalleague.org/adopt-a-pet/dogs/mixed-breed-rescue-and-adoption-mutt-i-grees.html

This animal rescue is located in New York state.

- **Dog Breed Info Center** Rescue Listings

  https://www.rescueinfocenter.com/awpcp/browse-categories/206/cavachon/.

  A great list of dogs available for adoption.

- **Adopt-a-Pet.com** by Purina

  http://www.adoptapet.com/dog-adoption

  Another listing of adoptable dogs.

- **M.I.T. Mixed Breed Rescue**

  http://mitmixedbreedrescue.com/

  Lists mixed breed dogs for adoption, including designer dogs such as the Cavachon

U.K. Resources:

- **Beaubichons**

  http://www.beaubichons.co.uk/Cavachon-Puppies.html

  Experienced breeders specializing in designer dogs.

- **Rescue Organizations in the U.K.**

  http://www.pets4homes.co.uk/

  A general listing of both puppies for sale and rescue dogs.

- **Stokenchurch Dog Rescue** – Mixed Breed
  http://stokenchurchdogrescue.org.uk/dogs/term/mixed-breed.
  A general listing of mixed breed dogs available for adoption.
- **Battersea Dogs and Cats Home** – Breed Rescues
  http://www.battersea.org.uk/
  A listing of rescues across the U.K.

Canadian Cavachon Breeders:

http://www.spruceridgekennels.com/bichon-cross/cavachon
Located in Ontario

http://www.localpuppybreeders.com/cavachon-puppies-for-sale-in-canada/
A comprehensive list of reputable breeders located throughout Canada

https://www.kijiji.ca/b-dogs-puppies/canada/king-charles-puppy/k0c12610
A listing of various Cavalier King Charles designer dogs in Canada

Rescue Listings for Canada:

https://www.happytailsrescue.ca/
This rescue is located in Ontario, and it caters to a wide variety of designer or mixed breed dogs.

http://www.tpdr.ca
Tiny Paws Dog Rescue Canada - Another great source for finding a designer dog available for adoption.